# Language Arts 2 Copywork

All-in-One
Homeschool

This is just the copywork from
Language Arts 2
Easy Peasy All-in-One Homeschool.

This was created for the sake of convenience. Where in the online course it says to copy certain words or sentences, those have been included here. I hope this helps your family.

Copyright 2016
Editor Lee Giles
ISBN-13: 978-1515088844
ISBN-10: 1515088847

I think tongs look like

_____

_____

_____

_____

_____

_____

# Day 7

I was pulling weeds in my garden and noticed something unusual sticking up out of the dirt.

_____

_____

_____

_____

_____

_____

The cat she walks on padded claws. The wolf on the hills lays stealthy paws.

_____

_____

_____

_____

_____

_____

My clothes are soft and warm, fold
upon fold, but I'm so sorry for the
poor out in the cold.

_____

_____

_____

_____

_____

_____

# Day 13

If all were sun and never rain,
There'd be no rainbow still.

_____

_____

_____

_____

_____

_____

# Day 14

Stroke a flint, and there is nothing to admire: Strike a flint, and forthwith flash out sparks of fire.

_____

_____

_____

_____

_____

_____

# Day 15

If a pig wore a wig,

_____

_____

_____

_____

_____

_____

# Day 16

What will you give me for my pound? Full twenty shillings round.

_____

_____

_____

_____

_____

_____

_____

# Day 20

Boats sail on the rivers,
And ships sail on the seas;
But clouds that sail across the sky
Are prettier far than these.

_____

_____

_____

_____

_____

Now it is a very unusual thing for Mr. Toad to hurry, very unusual indeed.

_____

_____

_____

_____

_____

_____

# Day 27

You know Peter is always ready to go anywhere or do anything that will satisfy his curiosity.

_____

_____

_____

_____

_____

_____

# Day 29

He envies the birds because they can pour out in beautiful song the joy that is in them.

_____

_____

_____

_____

_____

_____

# Day 31

"What was the use of wasting my breath?" demanded Old Mr. Toad.

_____

_____

_____

_____

_____

_____

# Day 32

Oh, my, no!  No indeed!

_____

_____

_____

_____

_____

_____

"I'm just watching my babies.
Aren't they lovely?" said he.

_____

_____

_____

_____

_____

_____

# Day 34

"Why, I couldn't do that!" he exclaimed right out loud.

_____

_____

_____

_____

_____

_____

# Day 39

Write words with the –OR sound.

_____

_____

_____

_____

_____

_____

# Day 40

fire, pie, dial, pile, light, bicycle, by, bye, guide  Add 2 more.

_____

_____

_____

_____

_____

_____

# Day 41

Write words that rhyme with bare and that are spelled __A-R-E.

_____

_____

_____

_____

_____

_____

# Day 65

He stopped and into his yellow
eyes crept a look of suspicion.

_____

_____

_____

_____

_____

_____

# Day 67

oil, boil, coin, noise, noisy, avoid, choice, point

_____

_____

_____

_____

_____

_____

Jimmy Skunk was smiling as he ambled towards the old house of Johnny Chuck.

_____

_____

_____

_____

_____

_____

# Day 72

Ah have mo' important things to worry about. (Write in proper English.)

_____

_____

_____

_____

_____

_____

# Day 73

Prickly Porky and I are armed for defence, but we never use our weapons for offence.

_____

_____

_____

_____

_____

_____

# Day 97

The bride looks like a queen.

_____

_____

_____

_____

_____

_____

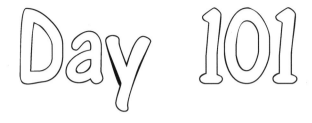

# Day 101

"But why do you carry that door?"
asked the sheriff.

_____

_____

_____

_____

_____

_____

# Day 112

"The man who has made up his mind to win," said Napoleon, "will never say impossible."

_____

_____

_____

_____

_____

_____

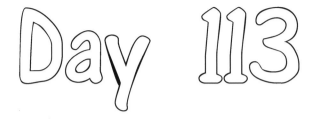

# Day 113

At first the Romans, who were very proud and brave, did not think there was much danger.

_____

_____

_____

_____

_____

_____

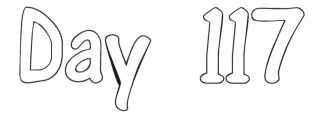

# Day 117

Nearly two thousand years ago there lived in Rome a man whose name was Julius Caesar.

_____

_____

_____

_____

_____

_____

# Day 122

## Alexander the Great

_____

_____

_____

_____

_____

_____

# Day 124

Genghis Khan's hawk

_____

_____

_____

_____

_____

_____

# Day 141

brag city cot face goal gym

_____

_____

_____

_____

_____

_____

# Day 142

isn't didn't I've I'll you've I'm
I'd let's he's she'll

_____

_____

_____

_____

_____

_____

larvae bakery officer customs
dough ingredients recipe
attention customer

_____

_____

_____

_____

_____

_____

# Day 146

brick, trick, click, tick  +3 more

_____

_____

_____

_____

_____

_____

# Day 147

we will, I have, you are, he is, +2
(Write them as contractions.)

_____

_____

_____

_____

_____

_____

# Day 148

bravely cheerful fearless
loudness sadly slowly useless
hopeful kindness

_____

_____

_____

_____

_____

_____

ball fall small paw yawn soft

_____

_____

_____

_____

_____

_____

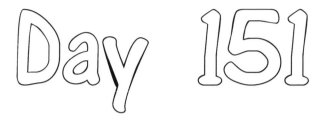

grumbled groaned fussed angry
promised grumpily penalty
advantage antennae

_____

_____

_____

_____

_____

_____

# Day 152

"I'm afraid I don't know how," replied the country lad.

_____

_____

_____

_____

_____

_____

# Day 153

"I'll have to teach Danny Rugg a good lesson," said Bert to his cousin.

_____

_____

_____

_____

_____

_____

# Day 154

"That's what we'll do!" cried Bert, steering toward it.

_____

_____

_____

_____

_____

_____

# Day 156

By this time the snowslide had reached the tree, and the mass was now much larger than at first.

_____

_____

_____

_____

_____

_____

# Day 159

Then came another thaw, and a freeze followed some days later, making good skating.

_____

_____

_____

_____

_____

_____

The Easy Peasy All-in-One Homeschool is a free, complete online homeschool curriculum. There are 180 days of ready-to-go assignments for every level and every subject. It's created for your children to work as independently as you want them to. Preschool through high school is available as well as courses ranging from English, math, science and history to art, music, computer, thinking, physical education and health. A daily Bible lesson is offered as well. The mission of Easy Peasy is to enable those to homeschool who otherwise thought they couldn't.

The Genesis Curriculum takes the Bible and turns it into lessons for your homeschool. Daily lessons include Bible reading, memory verse, spelling, handwriting, vocabulary, grammar, Biblical language, science, social studies, writing, and thinking through discussion questions.

The Genesis Curriculum uses a complete book of the Bible for one full year. The curriculum is being made using both Old and New Testament books. Find us online at genesiscurriculum.com to read about the latest developments in this expanding curriculum.

Made in the USA
Columbia, SC
21 August 2017